DEAR LEADERS,

HENRY AND ALEXAI ...U DEAD...

To Jo

With all good wishes

Sue Lownds

Sue Lownds

Pause for Space Publications

Published by Pause for Space Publications, 2008

Cover Design and Binding - Keele University

ISBN 0-9543662-4-7

For orders : please email:-

sue@thevanillaconcept.com

Pause for Space Publications - we specialise in quick read books.

Dedications

First and foremost for Kathy
who lives so many of the positive qualities
described and valued in these pages.

And for all those front line workers and managers
whose natural wisdom and generous words about their leaders
inspired this book.

Also for:-

- your talent for gathering together the best of teams - Barry A
- showing me, all those years ago, that excellent training is always about tuning in to your trainees and never about putting on a 'show' - Ralph L
- being the best of mentors - Brian C
- awesome thinking power - Sir John H-J
- your gift of transformational workplace coaching well before it became fashionable and for seeing the potential in me - Godfrey D
- your trailblazing - Chris R-D
- that most engaging and valuable combination of gifted perspicacity, undiluted realism and a wicked sense of the absurd - Maureen B
- being a leader of whom a bad word was never spoken - Gus A
- the confidence to be different - Richard A
- the far sightedness to break the mould - Richard S, Andy F

BEFORE YOU READ ON…

Dear Leaders

Sometimes we may feel bombarded with words of advice from the many management gurus, consultants, academics and specialists around the place. In these pages you will read the words of your own people. I hope you will find, as I did gathering them over the years, some of them for a research thesis, that, as John indicates on page one, the best modern organisational leaders are neither Henry V[th] nor Alexander the Great, but those who find the simplest of ways to gain, galvanise and sustain the contribution and success of their people.

You may also find that the stories here describe you, though you may well have taken some of these human qualities for granted in your search for leadership models. Some of my readers may be those of you who have so often told me that people are quick to criticise and slow to praise. Especially for you, I hope that the many, positive views in this volume go some way to redressing the balance.

We often take great account of the words of wisdom expressed by people at the top of organisations. The wisdom in these pages speaks for itself and is presented without further explanation since it needs none. It has come from those whose words are rarely quoted but should be, since they are the ones who make things happen for their leaders, day by day in the workplace. Their perspectives are generous, far sighted, humorous, optimistic, philosophical, filled with appreciation and admiration for the leaders who have inspired them, down to earth and occasionally stark and direct. All the comments are rooted in the experience of operational people, most in the front line of a range of organisations in both the public and private sectors. Their message to their leaders is this - if you want to inspire us, believe in and use your own ordinary human gifts.

They describe the type of leadership that does work for them and sometimes has not worked for them. In speaking so candidly, their words are pearls of inspiration for any organisational leader who cares really to listen.

Sue Lownds

My manager went on a course which I think was to show him how to be like Henry Vth or Alexander the Great or someone like that. Why make things so hard? My manager, along with so many others, is really rather good at engaging us in interesting discussions and conversations. You can hear this all around you, in the corridors, by the coffee machines or in the staff restaurant. If leaders want to inspire us, they just need to apply these natural skills to the workplace. The danger with organisations bigging up leadership is that they can fail to use the obvious, small things that are right under their noses.

John
Civil Servant

He comes into the restaurant at lunch time and there you'll see all the directors and senior managers clustered together and he looks around and comes and sits with us, the warehouse staff and the drivers who take his goods out to his customers. He asks us, and we tell him, what life is like for us and he tells us what life is like for him. Is that good sense or what?

Dave
Warehouseman

Solid foundations

Investing in the front line was the wisest thing he ever did. When the writing was on the wall, it was the foundations that kept the wall up

Peter
Stores Controller

How often do you hear our leaders say "Let's get our own house in order first before we share this or that with others" ?

I am lucky to be working for someone who inspires us by saying "Think about what you *can* do, not just what you have done and, if you have something good, use it for all you are worth because the opportunity may never come your way again and how will you feel if you end up saying 'If only I had had a go?' "

Confidence breeds confidence and the trusted repay the truster over and over again.

Lisa
Quality Manager

I've worked for loads of senior managers and I've never felt so confident about myself before. I've been a bit of an old cynic but this time we've got senior managers who are willing to go where their predecessors never dared. Being trusted and involved to make a difference as never before is like a turbo charger.

Neil
Civil Servant

Invented here = Buy-in

Our director announced that organisational change would only work when his front line had bought in. He then freed us up to take a lead in changing the way we work. Most of us were not used to this. The feeling that change wasn't being done to us set us free to influence our colleagues in a way that could never have worked if management had tried to do it.

John
Airport Engineer and Shop Steward

Excellence v Perfection

Some leaders need a route map. Ours have an internal compass and a belief in us that means new territory is exciting and worth exploring, not terrifying and mind numbing. They use the energy, willingness and good people they have. They set the ambition and we have been trusted to just get on with introducing our own improvements in our own workplaces and, interestingly, I would say we have set standards that probably exceed the ones they set initially.

That's what happens if you have leaders with the nerve to trust their own people to have a go at a new way of doing things. Those who aren't confident leaders wait for excellence to become perfection and have missed the chance of a lifetime because they are still waiting.

Vij
Construction Manager

There's a difference between bullying and straight talking and there are too many managers who run away from straight talking because they are scared of being accused of bullying.

My last team leader was very supportive but also very straight talking. One thing I will always remember her for is her attitude to the Friday/Monday absences that were beginning to become a pattern - "We are all taking money to do a job of work. If we don't do it properly, that's stealing."

Those of us working alongside people who rip the rest of us off appreciate that kind of straight talking.

Joan
Security Officer

My best work experience has been working for a woman who saw us, not the task, as her in-tray. If you are a leader of people, the only in-tray for you is your people, isn't it?

Mike
Airport Duty Officer

When you hire a plumber or any other craftsman, you don't tell him how to do his job. If my manager stands over me and tells me what to do, he must want to be me. Either the organisation doesn't need him or it doesn't need me. And I'm cheaper.

John
Engineer

Promotion dilemma

My manager always likes to describe himself as "a career investigator" and our director insists on reminding him - "No you are a manager of people and they are the career investigators." He is right!

David
Investigator

I joined the company thinking of myself as a technician. On my first day I attended the company induction session and I heard the CEO speak. It was the simplest of messages about my influence in shaping the good name and image of the company. I now think of myself as a company salesman who can mould the reputation of the company every time I speak to a supplier or a customer.

Anthony
Systems Analyst and 'Salesperson'

I admire my manager because I feel he acts in my interest. He admires me because I act in our customers' interests. I trust him to do right by me because he has proved he does. He trusts me to do right by our customers because I have proved I do. It's the best of partnerships.

Colin
Installation Engineer

We had a Question and Answer forum with our director. The most motivating aspect of it was when he spoke about our good work and said "you are my luck." What a simple, warm and motivating way to put it.

Sally
Customer Services

A simple request

The most impressive language I've heard in a long time from one of our directors is - "Tell me what I can do for you."

Jenn
Customer Enquiries

A risk is only a risk if you haven't got the right people. One thing I can say about my director is that he knows how to gather the right people together.

Jill
Sales Secretary

I've been twenty four years in this organisation and I've seen complexity increase. Umpteen competencies and codes. Surely there is only one thing that will really ensure we do our very best all of the time - pride. And that doesn't come from competencies and box ticking; it comes from being proud to be associated with someone. If every leader was that someone, they'll have cracked it.

My message to all our leaders? If you pore over competency lists, you are playing the bureaucrat's game. Spend more time using your normal, human skills. You'll find it's easy and works wonders.

Bill
Customer Service Supervisor

Something that matters a lot to our manager is his team's good name and reputation. That kind of emphasis is infectious and the safeguarding of our good name is pretty much in our own hands.

Jennifer
Expenses Clerk

My manager talks about "work ethic", "esprit de corps", "limitless vision," "legacy," and all this kind of stuff. Meanwhile, we wonder what the organisation is all about.

Joe
Photographic Sales

This time I am in a project where the whole purpose has been put into one goal - the date of completion. It's inspired. Instead of grand vision statements, it's crystal clear what we are about - successful completion by the date to which we've committed. How obvious and common sense is that?

Les
Construction Worker

We are at work so much, why would we not want it to be as good as possible? Leaders who don't see this and who don't use us to make our own workplaces fantastic are failing to use one of the easiest and most obvious things in their grasp.

Michael
Night Shift Leader

In organisational terms, pearls emerge whenever we lowly lot are encouraged by our leaders to see how influential we can really be. Since arriving here and working under a new director I've realised it's really not that hard to get us involved and giving an awful lot extra if we are just helped to see the possibilities for ourselves at a personal level.

Mark
Claims Processing

My experience of being in a project team led by a woman who holds a daily, informal conversation with us first thing each day has made me realise that, when our manager just takes a little time to connect with us on a day to day basis, not only are we all motivated by her informality and interest but she also has her finger on the pulse, nipping problems in the bud. And she picks up on all those many, many ideas for work improvement that operational people have every day but never bother to raise because it seems like too big a deal, or too pushy, to raise them formally.

Margaret
Accounts Clerk

I used to work for a woman who decided to bring in Danish pastries for our weekly planning meeting to give it a more relaxed feel. Her manager happened to walk in one day and told her off in front of us, saying that this kind of unorthodox thing was not needed. I'd say he missed the point. We were using informal conversation to kill several birds with one stone - all of them work related and all of them motivational.

She later went on to head up a major, well-known business and had a reputation for inspiring others. Yes, he missed the point!

Ken
Airline manager

From the heart

She stood up and just said to us off the cuff "I don't know what inspirational looks like but I know what it feels like and it feels like what you've just done." That was far more genuine and motivational than the most flashy of prepared speeches.

Andrew
Civil Servant

In my team we talk about the two ears - the tin ear that doesn't hear us and the flesh ear that does.

We probably all have tin ear moments when we are so focused on getting a task done that nothing else matters. But a permanent tin ear is a hopeless leader.

I get a lot from being listened to, even if it has to be a formal forum or something like that once in a while. But the best of the best, in my opinion, is a leader who can do a complex job and still keep an ear open for what is going on around the patch.

One of the best leaders I have ever worked for used to record his ideas (or actually our ideas) as he walked around the place, meeting and chatting informally with people. It was something he did every month. He had a small team who used to look into these ideas and reported directly to him. Once I was consulted about something I had said about overlap communication between shifts. He'd made a record of this and got his team to look at it. I received a note of thanks and gift vouchers. But I was more proud of being told I had made a difference.

Stanley
Engineering Despatcher

If there is one thing we do in order processing it is keep the customer happy. No one who works in this department wants to have customer hassle each day. We make sure, for our own sanity and work enjoyment, that we do whatever we have to in order to get an order out accurately and on time. When you have a manager who understands that, it is like soaring. When you have a manager who doesn't, you get all kinds of constraints and rules that may be great for a command and control mentality but do nothing for the customer.

I think I am lucky now to work with a team leader who seeks out our ideas and appreciates our experience. In the past I have worked in a situation where the hundreds of years of collective experience that we had in the team counted for nothing and we ended up with a work process of doing pieces of things with no sense of the whole service we were supposed to be delivering. It was a horrendous "do what you are told" period where accuracy went down and so did customer patience, and sick leave went up because people couldn't stand all the hassle.

Karen
Order Processor

Followers = people who *want* to be there with you

If someone says - "I know you have good experience. I know you have good ideas. Let's hear them."
If someone says - "What would you need to put those good ideas into practice? I'll help you."
If someone says - "Thank you for doing something that has really helped."
If all our managers say and do these things, well then we'll get up each day looking forward to coming into work instead of enduring it because we have to earn a living.

Joanne
Marketing Executive

Top managers aren't the only people leading life like a speeded up film. Most of us do. In my team, not only is our service in high demand, but we are also mostly parents of young children outside work. Sometimes the pressure of juggling grows and our service slips.

One day our senior manager was visiting and asked us what we would do to make the service as good as possible. We came up with the suggestion that each one of us would have one day a month catching up on our backlog and doing our work planning at home. We would cover for each other.

Most senior managers here are paranoid about home working, believing it to be a charter for skivers. In fact, for this reason, I don't think what we are doing has ever been formalised. We are lucky to have a leader who is prepared to buck the trend. I can't remember the last time any of us took any sick absence.

Anne
Communications Team

My manager is a fanatical gardener and he often makes us laugh with his gardening analogies. But sometimes they make you think. At one of our sales team briefings he gave an amusing talk about the value of the earthworm that leaves castings eight times its weight everyday. He encouraged us all, like the earthworm, to make the most of what comes naturally to us. Building strong customer relationships leaves castings of goodwill and a good reputation along our way that feed and nourish business success.

Lynne
Account Manager

How great to be led by someone for whom your grade is irrelevant. I used to work in an organisation where, in every training course, when people were asked to introduce themselves, they would say their grade!

Our team is an example of people who are not usually noticed - many of us are from the bottom rungs. Our section leader never, never refers to grade. What this means to me, personally, is that I feel confident about putting forward my ideas and I think I could say that nobody here is fearful about talking about what is not going so well. It is like everyone has something to learn from everyone else.

Whether that's leadership, I don't know, but I think everyone here *wants* to be here.

Jane
Security Officer

Eye on the prize

It's not much use these days telling us we have to drench ourselves in work in order to succeed. We all have lives outside. If the only people to get on are those who commit 200% all the time then the business is missing out on a whole lot of talent.

My inspiration comes from people like our Customer Services Director who spoke to us yesterday and said "Our success and the delight of our customers are one and the same. We don't have to work all hours to delight our customers if every new process or policy we introduce has a positive answer to the question 'And does this make things really good for our customer?'. If the answer is 'It doesn't' and we still go ahead, then we are doing things for our convenience and not for them. And if, as a business, we do things for our own convenience, we are doomed."

Janet
Human Resources Business Partner

It is OK sometimes for leaders (and the rest of us) to tell the well poisoners to shut up and move on.

Jeanette
Interim Manager

Our director personally makes us feel welcome and needed - not every day, that's not possible, but every time she comes across us - in the lift, or the lobby or queuing up for lunch. It sounds like a small thing but how good it makes you feel.

Contrast that with our new Chairman. I introduced myself to him and he said "Do I need to know this?" Any leader who acts as though common courtesy is an irrelevance is past his sell by date because you can't command or demand obeisance - those days are gone.

Irene
Board Support

Talent goes where it is valued

I work for a manager who constantly has people beating a path to her door. That may be because we all talk about how she values us.

Phil
Learning Advisor

We have so many good people and managers. So why do we reach for consultants so often?

Claire
Civil Servant

Why not?

Our Director often does his "Why not?" speech.

We have an idea - why not say it?

We see the solution to a problem - why not share it?

We see something working well - why not copy it?

We see a poor job being done - why not challenge it?

Anna
Claims Assistant

I can't get involved in extras at work unless I believe in them. The skill of my manager is that she knows the words to help me to see that I believe in them. I end up getting involved all the time.

Judith
Customer Hotline

My manager tends to challenge my 'play safe' mentality. At my last appraisal she said "It's no good saying 'If only' when all the time you could have taken a bit of a risk and succeeded beyond expectations." It makes me feel she sees possibilities in me that I may not see in myself. It's so motivating to know you are working for someone who shows that she really believes in you and encourages you to believe in yourself.

Anne
Accountant

We are confident about our ideas being heard. We are always being told - "If you know a better way of doing this, please tell me."

Jonathan
Data Processor

My Director says we don't owe him a living.

Sam
Medical Sales

When our managers talk about being 'on message' they mean sticking to the party line. To me being on message is being truthful to the customer. It seems to me that the real skill of leadership is making sure no one ever has to lie to a customer because of an unsuitable process or an unsuitable person appointed to a task.

Mitch
Pensions Administrator

You can be very, very nice and very, very successful - I work for someone like this.

Angela
PA to Director, Cost Consultancy

I smile when I hear the words "people are our greatest assets." Look, we can take it. We know we are goods and chattels and that, when the world moves on, we can be dumped. Be honest about it. We'll understand. Then just help us to get ready for that moment. That's far more honest.

Philip
Warehouse Supervisor

The word challenge should make us feel excited. It shouldn't make us feel that our leaders haven't the faintest.

Bob
Stock Controller

One of our directors used to like conferences where he'd make us indulge in so-called 'fun'. Once he had us behaving like a bunch of cowboys in some Wild West scenario. I'm sure it would have cost a fortune to put these things on and we all went along with it because we felt we had to, but all the time thinking less and less of him.

Rick
Project Supervisor

More is less

Earth has one moon, Saturn has 60. Leaders may see thousands of opportunities, but showing us that one moon that we can all reach is one of the most inspiring things.

Thinking 70 light years ahead

70 light years away aliens would just be seeing TV pictures of Hitler. Farseeing leaders are our security. It is in our interest to work with them.

Robin
Training Manager and Amateur Astronomer

We used to have a company 'kick off' conference every January which would involve all kinds of games and larking about devised by people who like that kind of thing. It took no account of those who didn't like that kind of thing and the feeling you got was "fit in or f*** off." Hardly inspirational.

Sam
Credit Control

Our Managing Director got someone to devise a company song. It made us feel we were back in school and people looked embarrassed for themselves and for him. Motivation can't be something contrived like that. It was a shame because actually he is someone we all like and he is good at praising our successes. Sometimes you can get carried away and lose sight of the power of simplicity.

Sandie
Credit Analyst

They should take a look at our loos - if our senior managers had to use these toilets they'd soon improve.

George
Construction worker

It isn't clever when top leaders tell us to co-operate and share and then don't do these things themselves. My best leader was a man who was big thinking enough to lead people out of their silos which only flourish if the very top lets them.

Jack
Finance Clerk

You can't be a leader if you let the jobs-worths rule the roost. It drags us all down.

Andy
Civil Servant

Unbridled trust is naïve. Of course people will lie to save their skins. It's good to be trusted, of course it is, but wise leaders will always have a system of checking up, even if it isn't obvious.

Jack
Warehouseman

I love working with my current manager. She isn't hide bound by processes. She sees them as guidance to use when we are unsure but, when we are sure of what we are doing, she trusts us to deliver. How we get there is up to us as long as we do get there and to the standards she expects. My last manager used to get frazzled and was always saying "You are working out of process" as though the process was more important than a good result.

Ruth
Sales Support

Being seen matters

We saw so little of him that we thought he was a cardboard cut out.

Ben
Engineer

There's a lot of contrived controversy in shows like The Apprentice and Dragons' Den but, to me, that isn't business - I look upon these programmes as great entertainment. If you are rude and disrespectful of people in real life, do you really think they will pull out all the stops for you when you most need them? Or do you think they'll take the first opportunity to cut your legs off?

Rachele
Customer Help Desk

I've heard that most people organise their thoughts in threes. I think we must be led by an exceptional person. She organises her thoughts in fours and fives. She is full of ideas and concepts but explains them so simply and logically that it is clear where she is leading us and what are the stepping stones. If only all strategic thinkers could do the same.

Jackie
Marketing

The boiling frog

An autocratic, centralised leadership style is old fashioned and ineffective when all around the leadership there are bright, intelligent people who can do so much on their own initiative. Organisations that foster this kind of hierarchical leadership are like the proverbial boiling frog - sitting in the pan, lulled into a feeling of false security, not realising the water is heating up and that it will soon boil to death.

Susan
Product Design

There is something wrong when the bullies and show-offs are rewarded. It's the generous people that inspire us, not the asses.

Mike
Management Accountant

Senior managers need to take care when commissioning training. We had a bloke talk to us about the Earth being in F Sharp. Imaginative language is catchy but it also needs to make sense to the mass of people who don't think this way. Most of us are grounded and practical and we need grounded and practical words.

Steve
Claims Supervisor

The past is gone. The present and the future are in our interest. Our leaders don't find us harping on about the past whenever they have made (and helped us to make) the present something to enjoy and the future something to long for.

Nigel
Telephone Orders

Leaders who inspire are those who see their personal rewards tied up in us, their people.

Keith
Porter

We are led by a calculating machine. Unfortunately, calculating machines only make inspiring leaders if they also have the 3i quality - Imagination, Interest, Instinct. The imagination to put themselves in the shoes of others, a genuine interest in doing so and, above all, the instinct that tells them that, for their own good as well as the good of the business, they need to do so.

Margaret
Operations Manager

I think one of the important things for any leader is to make sure we don't bury our heads in the sand. We all need to be ready for tomorrow and tomorrow's skills may not be today's skills. Why are there not more topical discussions about the future of our business, led by our leaders - not at their exalted levels but at ours?

Con
Procurement Team

Behavioural inefficiency

The Head of our division often talks about behavioural inefficiency. He is the only leader around here whose emphasis is on behaviour and working relationships rather than system or process. If relationships are good, people will always find a way to make things work, even in the toughest of circumstances, because our instinct is to take responsibility for each other. But if relationships are bad, even the best processes will let us down.

Wendy
Law Enforcement

A productive relationship

If you know what I am like I'll be very easy to manage.

Judy
Senior Secretary

Honesty wins admiration

When it comes to your own team, there is no such thing as trimming the truth. It's a dead cert for leadership failure.

Brian
Despatch Team Leader

Some people think that change at work is like camouflage - a sort of temporary thing. I'm really pleased to be working for a director who takes the time, regularly, to remind us how much we have changed in ourselves, for ourselves and by ourselves in our lives. When you are encouraged to see yourself like that, work change seems like a most natural and normal thing and something for which we are all skilled and ready.

Anna
Assistant to Airport Manager

Stunted

When is change leadership a stunt? When leaders' words don't match their behaviour.

Gordon
Quantity Surveyor

I was once given the advice that careers can't stand still - if they are not moving forward, they are moving backwards because the rest of the world will soon overtake us. Most of us can see ourselves moving on, we can see our colleagues moving on and we can see our leaders moving on, but we don't see our organisations that way and that's maybe why people feel unsettled every time we have a change of organisational structure. We all need a bit of the vagabond in us - perhaps that's something our leaders should actively encourage.

Jake
Internal Communications

Leaders who place too much reliance on convention, traditional hierarchies and external consultants hobble their organisations.

Mo
Civil Servant

I love the clarity I get from my senior manager.

Who we are

What we are here for

How we do it

Mary
Front Office manager

The stone hunters

We seem to be in the age of the stone hunters - all our top managers searching under every guru's stone for the secret of leadership. If you want to know about leadership, ask us, ask the led.

Gareth
Telesales

It's refreshing to work for an organisation that doesn't pretend to want to keep us no matter what. Times change and talent development shouldn't just be focused on going up; it should also focus us on going out. Fresh blood makes for fresh organisations and fresh experience freshens up people and their prospects.

Carolyn
Marketing Services

Success is succession. I am fortunate to work for a leader who knows and acts on this.

Anthony
Cost Consultant

Do we really have to be called 'human capital'? If we are human capital, does that make our leaders human traffickers?

Keith
Photographic Technician

Self-assessment flaws

There's a limit to self-assessment questionnaires. My leader sees himself as a risk taker but clings to the rule book.

Sue
Customer Queries

Mood

Attitude surveys are a once-in-a-while mood check. That's all. They are no substitute for leaders getting right in amongst us for themselves. This is the first time I have worked for an organisation where the top man drops in unannounced - no red carpet, no advance plans, nothing. Go around and see if you hear any of the staff bad mouthing him. You probably won't. How can you sensibly quantify the business benefits of that?

Janine
Fleet Administrator

Growing up

In this organisation, we seem to be stuck with old behaviours. The world has moved on from paternal managers who 'know best'.

John
Electrician

What's with this term 'pink and fluffy' anyway? It helps us to build sensible working relationships precisely in order to tackle productivity, coasters, plodders, low performers, low capability, runners away from progress. How come that's considered fluffy?

Carol
Sales Manager

Pink and fluffy is not for sissies. It's about having the plain good sense really to invest in sometimes difficult and contentious working relationships with everyone who works on your behalf. Not to do so is to consign your business to the vagaries of superficial and uninspiring leadership.

Helen
Consultant Engineer and Team Leader

Reducing your people to a mass of figures and statistics and targets is a pretty bankrupt way to lead but a great treat for a backroom boy.

Jock
Stock Controller

There is a difference between using time and using up time. Corridor conversations are about building relationships. Leaders who don't understand this don't understand that relationships make business work.

Joely
Education Department

Chatting to my colleagues and my customers is not about not working. It's about working to build up a network of mutual responsibility for what we all have to deliver in this business. It means we are more likely to help each other out. Isn't that good for business?

Diane
Airport Duty Manager

Shit happens and there are times when shit can make things happen. Sometimes leaders have to just say it like it is. And sometimes we all have to hear it like it is.

Andrew
Site Maintenance

I work for an amazing woman. Never for a moment does she slavishly follow what others are doing. Whenever some directive or new fad comes out, she looks at whether it will be right for us. For example, we were told that all our training had to be computer based. Well, that did not suit all of us in the team. So she ran the training herself and trained up one of us to take it on, too. We told her that the very thought of the company's assessment centres made us feel like rats in a lab, so she took us through the whole process stage by stage, asking us to rewrite some of the criteria in our language so that we could see why we were being put through this. I don't think there is a single person here who would not give a whole lot more to our work because of her.

Ronnie
Facilities Services

The worth of first impressions

Leaders have difficult judgements to make but I often wonder why receptionists, the first people to greet valued and important customers, are amongst the lowest paid.

Ashok
Office Manager

I view my manager as a real role model and a benchmark of how I would wish to be when I get into management. She personally inducts newcomers, she has contact with us every day, she advises, monitors, counsels, develops, informs us and she looks ahead to remind us what may be coming. When I look across to other teams, I feel sorry for them and glad for us.

Veronica
Logistics Team

The Rat Race

I once heard someone say that the trouble with being in the rat race is you are still a rat. We have all kinds of diversity targets for the so called 'under represented' groups in government but many of us look up and just see unhappy rats. Making life in the upper echelons attractive probably needs a family feel but people at the top are in a rat race they can't seem to control. A leader who can break through that won't need breakthrough diversity targets.

Reeta
Civil Servant

One of the best things now is working for a woman who is prepared to break with the convention of our organisation and use her most junior staff as her ideas generators. We know what works for our customers and she's willing to trust our judgement and our suggestions. In working this way she has also made us her personal ambassadors. I think that's clever leadership.

Gloria
Shift Leader

I work for a manager who knows how far to go in helping so that it doesn't feel like interfering, and how far to go in being flexible so that he doesn't come across as wishy washy, and how far to go in being thorough so that he doesn't come across as fanatical.

Lucy
Order Processor

When our managers speak in our language we always do things right first time.

Pete
Fork Lift Driver

If you take the trouble to talk to us, we can say 'this works' and 'this doesn't.'

Paul
Office Maintenance

If you don't stay in touch with us, sometimes a mistake won't come to light for months.

Karen
Canteen Supervisor

People don't sabotage if they understand and the best leaders, in my experience, take the time and trouble to make sure we all do. Some things are best not delegated.

Freda
Traffic Help Desk

If promotion results only from self-marketing, we could miss out on the excellence of modest people.

Judith
Personal Coach

Out dated?

If macho was the secret of great leadership, no organisation would suffer from absence.

Kit
Warehouse Manager

360° apart

I think 360° feedback keeps our leaders apart from us. I work for a woman who simply sits with us and asks us for feedback. We are able to discuss her and she is able to discuss us. If some managers need help to be able to do it this way, then give them the help. It seems to me to be a far more grown up way of behaving than hiding behind anonymous 360° appraisals.

Len
Sales Assistant

I was asked to complete an online questionnaire to help me, as a leader, to become inspirational. The tool, we were told, was designed after interviews with 40 leaders. To me this is rather missing the point. Leadership is human not intellectual and if I am to be an inspirational leader, it's my people who should be commenting, not me.

David
Civil Servant

Bald stats

Where I work people take an average of 30 days of sick leave - that's like each person being given an extra month of paid holiday each year. Do you think there could be a connection with leadership style?

Don
Security

Competency frameworks seem to me to be a shelter for mediocrity. Long lists of competencies are actually letting us off the hook. We can hide in the trees and our leaders aren't really getting what they need from us, but, if they are of a bureaucratic mindset, they would think they are.

Al
Personal Assistant

Reality

Sometimes leaders just need to be brave enough to remind people that we come to work to work and that we all take money for what we do.

Malcolm
Help Line

I report to someone who has managed to make productivity addictive. She is a great motivator, creating productivity from the different ways in which we are each allowed to work because she has bothered to find out what makes us each tick. Feeling motivated is addictive - in my view, good leaders would know that.

Marilyn
Civil Servant

Confidence is its own armour

The real boost my manager provided was my self-confidence. He did this through a planned programme of developing us as individuals and as a team, personally testing our technical knowledge and our influencing skills, like medics have 'vivas.' Confidence comes from being sure of what you are doing. Confident people don't need protection. I often wonder, for example, why we are told never to give out the names of our directors. Confidence needs no hiding place.

Jacob
Customer Complaints Team

Turmoil can be terrific if you make it in our interest.

Alan
Pharmacist

One pixel

Even if we only work on one pixel of the mega picture, we can still feel so good about our contribution whenever we are led by people who can paint that picture vividly.

Samantha
Administrative Assistant

I am required to fill in a time log every 15 minutes. How can you be innovative and far thinking in a mire of monitoring madness?

Elaine
Clerk

Being released by our director to act on our own improvement ideas without having to ask for permission every step of the way was like the City of Bath welcoming the disruption of archaeological digging to show its special place on the Fosse Way. You accommodate any disruption because you are so thrilled to be special.

Stephen
Tax Specialist and Amateur Archaeologist

I feel safe with my manager. He has never been a leader who stampedes towards a way of doing things just because everyone else is. He says that's the way you get mown down.

Juliet
Board Secretary

No vicious circle

Letting go was one of the brightest and bravest things our director did. As a front line coach, I feel trusted because I'm capable and capable because I have been trusted.

Mark
Operational Coach

Why do our top managers think leadership is some kind of mysterious and incredible skill? It is simply being human and all those talented people selected for leadership roles should be able to be that, shouldn't they?

Jennifer
Compensation and Benefits Specialist

Sadly I am led by a man who loves his PC more than his people.

Faith
Passenger Services

I work in a team where we have been encouraged to take ownership of our work no matter what. You won't find people here blaming systems failures. PCs don't communicate, telephones don't communicate, files don't lose themselves or lock themselves shut. We do.

Catherine
Premises Supervisor

My manager places great emphasis on decent etiquette.

A kind word.

A smile.

An acknowledgement.

Sticking to appointments.

Normal etiquette and courtesy.

Each of these makes her more and more the kind of person for whom we would stick our necks out.

Caity
Civil Servant

Young leaders can be exciting and stimulating whenever they value the wisdom of their elders and, especially, when they listen to those people right at the bottom of the ladder who happen to have years and years of experience on the ground and are there, ready to help the leader who notices them.

Harry
Process Improvement Team

The afternoon nap

You know absence is like the Spanish siesta. People are recharging because the workplace isn't a recharging place to be.

Outside of work many of us do extraordinary things and take lots of responsibility in our lives. Our manager has now discovered all the gumption we use outside work and has started to involve those skills.

Perhaps we'll find, as work becomes an invigorating place to be, absence will disappear.

Kim
Clerk

Talk to us at the most significant time. Do an induction refresher after nine months or so and ask us then how we are feeling about things and what could be better. Timing is everything.

Dan
Delivery Driver

If their behaviour is louder than their words, our leaders shouldn't be surprised if we don't hear what they may desperately want us to hear.

Corinne
Invoices Clerk

Being one of the lads is not the same as connecting with the lads. I was amazed to see two top directors, one male and one female, on the platform at our staff conference trying to out-talk each other about which one was likely to get drunk first. It was a huge misjudgement.

Dennis
Contracts Administrator

It's inspiring to hear our senior manager talk about us as his hands and eyes and ears without which he couldn't function at all.   The inter-relationship between all of us is something about which he is passionate and each of us - the hand or the eye or the ear - is a gift to the whole.

Janet
Marketing Executive

I have worked for years on building sites in the construction industry. One day, a group of us were invited to meet the boss man from the client organisation who had decided he would like to talk directly to those of us who were working on site. He spent a good hour with us, asking us what made our work tick over well and what areas we thought could be bettered. We felt pretty good that someone like him had bothered to take the time.

Soon after this, I had the opportunity to talk to my own senior manager and I suggested he could also take some time to talk to the site workers. "What would I say to them?" was his reply. I said "I don't think you'll have to say very much - they'll have plenty to talk about, if you show you are interested." "And what do you think would happen to my day job if I spent my time talking to site workers?"

I didn't have the nerve to say what I thought of that attitude.

Dileep
Construction Worker

Life in the tree tops

If leaders think of themselves as the top of the tree and confine their communication to the top, they are in danger of dying of thirst, disconnected from the root system.

Anil
Civil Servant

I wrote a letter to one of the Board directors. I told him about some of the great work that was going on in the front line of the corporation and I asked him to speak to those who were doing such great stuff. I told him they would be uplifted by the unexpected contact from a man they did not come across in their daily work, a man that was viewed with awe. Do you know what he did? He got his secretary to write a letter and he signed it. Then he asked his director in the line to take note of what I had said, desperately hide bound by a hierarchical instinct from which he could not break free. All he needed to do was to pick up the 'phone to one of those special people and say 'thank you.' It would have transformed his reputation.

I don't believe it was his fault. Sometimes the best response, even in the most kind and well meaning of leaders, is lost in the fog of bureaucratic tradition which binds people to a way of doing things that misses the opportunity of the moment. It takes real gumption and a different way of thinking to break out. If leaders want to amaze and inspire, they should *do* something non hierarchical. The resulting appreciation will outstrip any formal PR.

Paul
Professional Services

When our leaders bother to take the time to get to know us, they find that they can ask for a lot of commitment from us and get even more.

Jennifer
PA to Construction Director

Why would leaders think we are not on their side? We are. Everything they do really well has a wonderful impact on us. So why would we not want them to do well?

Matt
Customs Officer

When I was quite new to the world of work, I quickly learned that the leaders who believe in their own people are most likely to give us a chance to do things that extend our own opportunities as well as the business and then ... well, the world is their oyster, and ours, surely.

Martha
Retail Manager

About The Author

Sue Lownds has worked in the field of personal and organisational development for twenty five years and, together with her husband, Ken, runs a learning and development consultancy. Sue is a Fellow of the Chartered Institute of Personnel and Development who has researched and written about the link between leadership style and front line success.

Also by Sue Lownds:-

Fast Track to Change

The Vanilla Concept

www.thevanillaconcept.com